My Local Government

Denny O'Nan

ROSEN
COMMON CORE
READERS

Rosen
Classroom™

New York

Published in 2014 by The Rosen Publishing Group, Inc.
29 East 21st Street, New York, NY 10010

Book Design: Katelyn Londino

Photo Credits: Cover, p. 7 (Buffalo City Hall) jiawangkun/Shutterstock.com; pp. 3–24 (background) Olaru Radian-Alexandru/
Shutterstock.com; pp. 5, 9 Digital Vision/Thinkstock.com; p. 7 (city council meeting) http://en.wikipedia.org/wiki/
File:Fullerton_City_Council.jpg/Wikipedia.org; p. 11 Peter Baxter/Shutterstock.com; p. 13 Kenneth Sponsler/Shutterstock.com;
p. 15 Steve Debenport/E+/Getty Images; p. 17 Don Mason/Blend Images/Getty Images; p. 19 Dmitry Kalinovsky/
Shutterstock.com; p. 21 Kamira/Shutterstock.com; p. 22 (girl presenting) Lifesize/Thinkstock.com; p. 22 (writing a letter)
Ed Lemery/Shutterstock.com; p. 22 (kids picking up trash) Creatas/Thinkstock.com; p. 22 (voting) Andrey Burmakin/
Shutterstock.com; p. 22 (city council) VladKol/Shutterstock.com.

ISBN: 978-1-4777-2572-6
6-pack ISBN: 978-1-4777-2573-3

Manufactured in the United States of America

CPSIA Compliance Information: Batch #CS13RC: For further information contact Rosen Publishing, New York, New York at 1-800-237-9932.

Contents

My Community

I love the community I live in! It has all the things I need and want, such as schools, libraries, and parks. Lately, I've wondered how my community works. How does it provide all those great services? Who's in charge of making decisions?

My teacher, Mr. Parker, tells me the best way to learn about a community is to learn about local government. My local government shapes the community and affects my everyday life.

Mr. Parker knows a lot about local government.
He says it's important to ask questions.

Local Government

I've already heard a lot about government in class. There are three major kinds of government: national, state, and local. The national government, led by the president, makes decisions for the whole country. The state government, led by the governor, makes decisions only for the state.

The local government takes care of anything the national and state governments don't. A mayor is usually the head of local government, and a **council** helps him. They make decisions only for their county, city, town, or village.

Most decisions and daily business in local government take place in city hall.

I take a trip to city hall to get more information on how my local government works. I learn that the mayor and council work together to make big decisions about laws and finances. They do this at city council meetings, which anyone in the community can attend.

I also learn that local governments make local laws. My community has a local law that says people can't let their dogs run loose, but not all communities have that law.

The leaders of local government are elected to their jobs. That means citizens vote for them.

Collecting Taxes

Local governments are **responsible** for collecting taxes from citizens. They use that money to pay for public services. One example of a public service **funded** by taxes is education. When I'm in school, I learn many important things that I'll need for my future, so I think this service is very important.

I also love to learn by reading books. The local government uses taxes to pay for public libraries. Libraries let me borrow books and use computers!

Because of public schools and libraries,
I can learn about anything!

My local government uses taxes to fund the public parks in my community. There's a big soccer park where all the teams can play. Soccer is my favorite sport, and I play on my town's soccer team every summer.

My government makes sure there are many things to do at public parks. There are sports, arts and crafts, and special events. Every year, my community has a big carnival in our park. There are so many fun things to do there!

I wonder how my community would have a carnival if they didn't collect taxes.

Keeping Us Safe

My local government also uses taxes to **protect** us. They hire police officers to keep citizens safe. Police officers make sure everyone in the community follows laws and treats others with respect. They also come into schools and teach kids about safety! I think this is very important.

The local government hires firefighters to keep citizens safe in emergencies, such as house fires. Firefighters use special trucks and tools to put out fires so people don't get hurt.

Officer Pratt is a police officer who sometimes comes into my class. He teaches us about making safe choices.

Cleaning and Fixing

Every Tuesday, my family fills trash cans and puts them in front of our house. Then, trash collectors stop by in their truck and take our garbage away. I know my local government uses our taxes to pay for this, too!

My local government pays for other ways to keep my community clean and safe. They hire people to clean parks and other public places. They also hire people to clean up water when it floods.

My Uncle John is a trash collector. He works for my local government to keep our community clean!

There's a construction crew on the street outside my school. There used to be holes in the road that were bad for cars. The government paid the construction crew to fix the road. My local government pays for traffic lights, too. It makes sure people can travel safely on the roads.

The government also pays for construction crews to build and **maintain** city buildings and other public spaces, such as the courthouse and beaches.

When construction crews fix roads and buildings, I think my community looks so much better!

What Can I Do?

There are many ways to get involved in local government. Next month, I can go to the city council meeting, which is where many big decisions are made.

Mr. Parker says I can write letters to city council members to discuss issues that are important to me. For example, I believe there should be new computers at the library. I think I'll write a letter to my local government about it soon!

The best part about local government is that everyone can get involved!

Kids Can Do It!

Getting Involved

teach others about local government

write letters to council members

help clean up parks

tell your parents to vote

go to city council meetings

Glossary

council (KOWN-suhl) A group of people chosen to make laws for a community.

fund (FUHND) To pay for.

maintain (mayn-TAYN) To keep in good condition.

protect (pruh-TEHKT) To keep safe.

responsible (rih-SPAHN-suh-buhl) Expected to take care of certain duties and jobs.

Index